THE RAUNDS STRIKE AND

MARCH TO LONDON

CENTENARY

(1905 – 2005)

by

JEROME BETTS

Illustrated and with a Map

Raunds and District History Society

The Society is indebted to the Heritage Lottery Fund, the Nationwide Building Society and the Countryside Agency for generous grants which have made this publication possible.

Published by Graham J. Underwood
22 Brooks Road
Raunds
Northamptonshire
NN9 6NS

ISBN 0-9550099-0-1
Design and typesetting by Graham Underwood
Manufactured in the U.K. by L.P.P.S. Ltd. Wellingborough, NN8 3PJ

DEDICATED

TO

ALL THOSE WHO TOOK PART

IN THE STRIKE AND MARCH OF 1905

By the same author.

The Raunds Strike and March to London 1905 (Booklet)

SB Published 1989

Second Edition 1991

Blessed Peter Wright S.J. – The Last Northamptonshire Martyr

HB Published 1998

CONTENTS

Appendices

LIST OF ILLUSTRATIONS

PAGE NO

Author's Preface and Acknowledgments

As a young child, visiting the home of my paternal grandparents, I became aware of three framed mementoes conspicuously displayed in one room of their cottage. At that time the significance of these faded images from the past was completely lost on me, although I was told my grandfather had been involved in some kind of demonstration. Only when I eventually inherited these objects did the realisation of their historical importance become clear. The largest of the three was a printed list of the 115 men who had marched to London in 1905 surmounted by a photograph of Councillor James Gribble of Northampton. The second object was a large posed photograph of all the men, taken some time after their return home, and in front of whom was a contingent displaying brass band instruments. The third and smallest frame contained a paper handkerchief showing a drawing of Trafalgar Square in London above which was the inscription; 'Souvenir of the Demonstration in Trafalgar Square of the Raunds Army Boot Makers.' These links with the past are still in my possession.

From an early age, I knew that my father, his two younger brothers and at least one of his sisters spent their working lives in the boot and shoe trade. In fact, the men of the family, including my grandfather, worked as operatives in the finishing room of Adams Brothers' boot factory in Gladstone Street Raunds. The making of boots for government departments, particularly the War Office, was the 'raison d'être' of this manufacturing enterprise as well as for about a dozen similar establishments scattered about in various parts of my home town. We were brought up within sight and sound of boot factories accompanied by the pungent smell of leather, most potent on Monday mornings when housewives burned leather bits to heat the water for the family wash. Whether it was these constant reminders of the staple trade, now alas defunct, which fostered a desire to find out more about the development of the boot and shoe industry, or an innate interest in things historical, is impossible to know.

However, I have first to thank my family ancestry for bringing the events of 1905 to my attention although they occurred more than twenty years before I was born. The late Mrs. Doreen Wright, a founder member and first secretary of the Raunds and District History Society, was also influential for suggesting I should present a lecture, in February 1989, on the subject of local history. The consequence was a description of the causes and events of the 1905 Strike and March, subsequently published as a pamphlet, which caught public imagination and sold almost fifteen hundred copies. Since then nearly forty lectures have been delivered by the author to a variety of societies throughout the county and beyond.

A decision to enlarge the booklet and produce a more extensive account to celebrate the centenary of the March was endorsed by the History Society Committee in 2003. The present publication, therefore, represents the result of diligent enquires by the author and other members of the Society particularly Mr. Roy Pentelow and Mr. Graham Underwood. I am also indebted to Mr. Paul Roberts for his knowledge of the shoe industry and historical research into the Nichols family.

Unfortunately, the experiences of those who took part in the events of 1905 were not recorded in any detail before they departed this life. Nevertheless, many newspapers and periodicals of the time are still preserved and have provided most of the information related in the present volume. The Northamptonshire

Record Office has been a rich source of newsworthy material, but I would also like to thank the staff of the Rushden Office of the Evening Telegraph for permitting me to spend many hours of research into an almost pristine collection of 1905 editions of the Wellingborough News.

The Secretary of the Northamptonshire Record Society, Mr. Leslie Skelton, has been pleased to allow free use to be made of Mr. Keith Brooker's article on James Gribble and the Raunds Strike printed in the 1981/82 edition of Northamptonshire Past and Present. Likewise, Messrs. Blackwell of Oxford have given permission to quote from Mr. Alan Fox's History of the National Union of Boot and Shoe Operatives published in 1958.

It would have taken many years to peruse all the relevant daily and weekly newspaper accounts of the Strike, and in particular the March. However, the notes and lists of sources found at the end of this book reveal that a comprehensive survey has been achieved. We cannot claim the account to be a complete or definitive history but rather an expanded version of dramatic events which, it is hoped, will give the reader a better understanding of the life and times of those who took part. Indeed, it was not inappropriate, in 1934, for Messrs. Allen and Bartley (see Reference Book list) to call the affair 'An Epic of Trade Unionism'. Their comments have also been incorporated in the text.

It only remains for me to thank Miss Jane Bailey for her typing skills and knowledge of computers, my wife for many hours of patient proof reading, and Mr. Graham Underwood for organising the publishing as well as sorting the illustrations. If I have missed anyone who should have been thanked, please accept my apologies. Any errors of fact or syntax are probably mine but I cannot be responsible for 1905 journalistic licence.

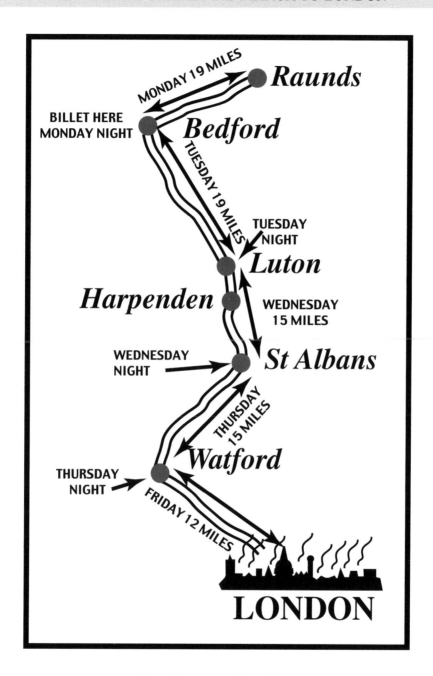

The Route to London

Abbreviations

D.N.B.	-	Dictionary of National Biography
E.T.	-	Evening Telegraph
K.C.	-	King's Counsel
N.M.	-	Northampton Mercury
N.P.P.	-	Northamptonshire Past and Present
N.R.O.	-	Northamptonshire Record Office
N.R.S.	-	Northamptonshire Record Society
N.U.B.S.O.	-	National Union of Boot and Shoe Operatives
S.D.F.	-	Social Democratic Federation

INTRODUCTION

The medieval settlement of Raunds covered a large scattered area which by the time of the first official census, in 1801, numbered 800 souls. One hundred years later, in 1901, the community had increased by a further 3,000 inhabitants and could quite correctly call itself a town by virtue of the 1894 Act of Parliament which had established a new governing body, the Raunds Urban District Council. By the end of the twentieth century, the town had been incorporated, together with a number of other small towns and villages, into the administrative district of East Northamptonshire.

Today, Raunds is a dormitory town of some 8,600 people but with only one major employer, engaged in the manufacture of plastic boxes. Most working townsfolk travel outside the district in cars and trains to places as diverse, and as distant, as London and Nottingham. Many of the newer residences are occupied by elderly folk, mainly from the London area, who have sought an affordable and quiet place in which to retire.

Yet, less than fifty years ago, when the population was only about 3,600, the town was all bustle and noise, reeking with the smell of leather. A dozen boot and shoe factories employed the majority of the population, both men and women. There was also a thriving tannery, a heel makers and a profitable clothing factory. All sorts of footwear was made; boots for the armed forces, boots for coal miners, firemen and policemen as well as sports footwear for leisure pursuits.

Boots had been made in Raunds for over two hundred years, perhaps even as far back as the seventeenth century when Oliver Cromwell ordered footwear, for his New Model Army, from the merchant suppliers of Northampton. Nearly all the Northamptonshire towns and villages had their local hand sewn craftsmen supplying boots to the merchants of Northampton during the late eighteenth and early nineteenth centuries. The army procurers in London preferred to buy from the county because the goods were cheaper than those made in London.

During the many wars of the eighteenth century the Army footwear industry became firmly established in the county at such places as Wellingborough, Kettering, Raunds, Daventry and Long Buckby as well as in Northampton itself. Partly as a result of the increase in demand and lower prices, by 1806, the county town was recognised as the principal shoe-making centre for the whole country[1]. As early as 1781 approximately 20 per cent of male workers in Raunds were employed as shoemakers. This was the highest proportion in the county apart from Wellingborough and Northampton[2]. By 1861 over six hundred men and women were recorded in the census as working in the shoe industry in Raunds.

There was clear evidence of superior organisation demonstrated by the statistic of almost 30 per cent of the population engaged in making mainly boots for the army. In fact, the company responsible for the beginnings of industrialisation was the brainchild of William Nichols. In 1829, he is listed, in a London Directory, as a Shoe Manufacturer of Raunds and Saint John Street, London[3]. Earlier, c.1826, Nichols together with his brother Thomas, originally farmers, had decided to by-pass the Northampton merchants by dealing direct with the government in

London, as wholesalers. [4]The partnership dissolved in 1829 and William took over as sole proprietor until 1873 when the Post Office Directory has the following entry[5]: "Nichols Wm. and Son, boot and shoe contractors, 13 Blackfriars Road, S.E." Other entries are to be found in Whellan's Directory, 1849, Kelly's Directory 1851, 1852, etc. with a final entry for 1886 at 111 Grays Inn Road, London, S.E. One can only suppose that the improvements made to the transport of goods by the railways, which first came to Northamptonshire in 1838 and finally reached Raunds in 1865, meant that an office cum warehouse in London was no longer required.

The firm employed a Raunds man, Thomas Beeby, as an agent in London from 1838 until c.1868. Nichols himself was not only an entrepreneur but something of an inventor who attempted to patent a novel lasting system for army boots in 1856 although the idea was never introduced. However, the Nichols family had a monopoly in Raunds for the manufacture of mainly army boots for more than fifty years. The son, John Knighton Nichols, became rich enough to build a brand new house, grandly called, 'The Hall', and had his own pack of hounds in kennels behind his factory premises. Today, 'The Hall' houses the offices of Raunds Council while the modern plastic container firm (R.P.C.) occupies the site of the former Nichols factory property although in modern premises.

The Nichols 'Empire' included shops selling groceries and drapery where, according to a letter of 1867 written by a shoemaker called Isaac Burton[6], the workers were expected to spend their wages. It is understood that the payment for work done was partly in money and partly vouchers to be spent in the company's shops[7]. The enterprise was very profitable for the employers as shown by the building of 'The Hall' and also the erection of the very large Methodist Chapel which still dominates Brook Street. The money for this imposing building was mainly donated by J.K.Nichols.

Of course, the monopoly exercised by the first large scale manufacturer in Raunds could not last for ever. J.K. Nichols died in 1893 but previously, in 1887, two of his foremen, brothers Owen Smith and John King Smith had set up a rival factory in Wellington Hill (later this became Wellington Tannery)[8]. Other men soon followed suit, so that by 1900 several manufacturers were operating from premises they had built in different parts of the town.

It must be clearly understood that these first factories did not equate, in any way, with the large new establishments already producing footwear for civilian use in the bigger towns of the county; Northampton, Kettering, Rushden and Wellingborough. At this time, and from as early as 1850, machinery for the stitching, riveting and making of boots and shoes had been introduced up and down the land; but this did not happen in Raunds until 1914.

In 1905, the factories in Raunds were merely warehouses where the clickers, who cut out the leather from patterns, together with the stockmen, were kept on the premises. Meanwhile the material for making was given out in baskets to individual boot makers who stitched the work by hand at home. A spare room might be utilised for the purpose or, more usually, a workshop at the end of the garden. The Raunds football team was nicknamed 'The Shopmates' as a result of this practice. The mode of employ was called basket work, for obvious reasons, or out work, and was traditional with the whole family involved. Wives and daughters hand stitched the uppers, by a method known as hand stabbing, while the men using wooden lasts, together with a multitude of tools, fixed the soles and heels, and finally finished off the boots.

Why did this 'cottage' industry persist for so long in Raunds? The answer is simply that the speciality of the town was the manufacture of service footwear, in particular army boots. Until just before the outbreak of the 1914 war, the War Office insisted, demanded might be a better word, that the boots supplied to them must be hand crafted, that is hand-sewn. It took a good man, with his family, to make eight pairs of boots per week, which fact was to be very important in the dispute which culminated in the Strike and March of 1905.

TRADE UNIONISM

Since it was the National Union of Boot and Shoe Operatives which organised the Strike (but not the March) it is important to trace the development of unionism during the nineteenth century. Before 1874, the only organisation representing the interests of the workers was the Amalgamated Cordwainers' Association, principally concerned with the interests of hand-sewn craftsmen. It had its roots in medieval England where the term Cordwainer denoted a worker in leather from Cordoba in Spain.

In 1874, a breakaway union was formed after a meeting at Stafford, attended by delegates from Northampton and many other parts of the country. The new union was called the National Union of Boot and Shoe Rivetters and Finishers[9]. By 1890 this had become the National Union of Boot and Shoe Operatives to embrace all who worked in the industry. With the closure of so many factories in the latter part of the twentieth century, shoe workers are now represented by the National Union of Knitwear, Footwear and Apparel Trades.

Until the last quarter of the nineteenth century the footwear industry was still largely cottage based using traditional hand-sewn methods. Gradually, however, the different processes required in making a pair of boots or shoes, that is clicking, rough stuff cutting, closing, lasting, sole and heel attachment and finishing, which had been achieved by one man and his family, became absorbed into a primitive factory system. The various operations were split up into three major divisions – clicking, closing and making, with men and women specialising in one of these now separate branches. Closing became an almost exclusive female occupation.

The Trade Union found it very difficult, at first, to organise the hand-sewn workers into any kind of association. If a man is busy in his own home, factory hours mean nothing, he can work for fourteen hours one day and only four the next, if he so wishes. Indeed, having been independent men for so long, working when they felt like it, the Northamptonshire shoemakers, or 'snobs', did not take kindly to regulations. There was a widespread tradition of 'fuddling', or going on the 'booze', at the weekend so that Monday was spent getting rid of the 'hangover'. In fact, Monday was known as Saint Monday, or 'Snobs' Monday, in most parts of Northamptonshire.

The new manufacturers, especially those with new machinery installed, began to make efforts to enforce factory hours and factory rules. The workers began to realise they needed a strong union to represent their interests. Although, by 1889, a start had been made in Raunds to recruit members, it was very slow progress. The resistance to unionisation was illustrated, in 1894, at the Union conference when a delegate from Stafford complained bitterly that a large navy contract had been placed in Raunds where non-union workers were prepared to do the job at a lower price[10].

This was an era of considerable unrest in the boot and shoe industry, such as the strike at St. Albans when workers demanded the 'outrageous' amount of thirty shillings (£1.50) per week. Before long, the Employers' Federation and the Union were locked in a dispute which escalated until 46,000 workers were either on strike or locked out. In Northamptonshire, the county town, Kettering and Rushden were badly affected with the Union losing half its membership. The Union had demanded the abolition of basketwork while the employers continued to use non-union labour.

In 1897 the Union representatives in Norwich demanded, more reasonably, a minimum wage of twenty eight shillings (£1.40) per week for clickers, twenty six shillings (£1.30) for pressmen and a fifty-four hour working week. After an eight month long strike which exhausted Union funds, the men were forced back to work without a recognised minimum wage or recognised hours of work.

The Union was in a worse state than before, with a continuous fall in membership nationally. Nevertheless, the advent of the Boer War (1899 - 1902) gave more work to the army boot makers of Raunds. For a short time, there was plenty of work and the statement price for making a pair of boots was strictly adhered to by both the contractors (manufacturers) and the War Office. Because of the rise in demand other contractors had also been tendering for the work in Northamptonshire notably at Finedon, Higham Ferrers, Irthlingborough, Kettering, Ringstead, Rushden and Wollaston.

However, when hostilities ceased there was an immediate fall in demand so that, as early as 1903, contractors began undercutting each other on prices in order to secure the few requisitions available. The War Office compounded the situation by not sticking to the agreed statement of prices which had previously been negotiated by the Union. The wages of employees in Raunds were drastically diminished. As early as January, 1904, a public meeting had been called by the chairman of the Urban Council which appointed an influential committee to canvas the town and organise relief for those families worst affected both by the lack of work and the low prices now being paid by the contractors. Strangely, some of the worst offenders in cost cutting were the businesses run by co-operative societies in Finedon, Ringstead,

Wollaston and, in particular, the St. Crispin Productive Society in Sackville Street, Raunds.

A deputation of councillors, not connected with the boot trade, was sent up to London to petition the War Office to try and secure more orders and to accept boots already made. Further meetings were held between Union officials and Mr. Bromley Davenport, Financial Secretary to the War Office, where it was definitely understood that the agreed statement of prices, already discussed, should be paid as in accordance with the fair wages clause of contracts[12].

That the above agreement was not honoured is shown by the following statement issued by Mr. W. Bazeley, secretary of the Rushden Branch of the Union :-

[13] *"The work for the ankle boots is being given out at one penny a pair for closing the backs and the counters. It takes a good closer ten hours to earn one shilling, and she herself has to find awls and bristles. The statement price for this operation should be two shillings and six pence per dozen.*

The ankle boot is being made and finished at two shillings and sixpence and two shillings and seven pence per pair, which is eight pence or nine pence under the proper statement price. It takes a good man to do eight pairs a week, and when he has done it at two shillings and seven pence, he earns not an unskilled labourer's pay.

On the cavalry boots, and all the work that is being made on the sectional system, it is being done at eight pence and nine pence per pair less than the proper statement price.

For mud boots, hand finished, the statement price is ten pence per pair but they are being given out at five pence per pair, or a reduction of fifty per cent."

The situation at Raunds which had been festering for more than a year, had now become acute. The General President of the Union, Mr. C. Freak, and the Secretary visited the district and interviewed one of the contractors (manufacturers). The interview was amicable but did not result in a satisfactory outcome.

Mass meetings of workers were held at Ringstead and in the Raunds Woodbine Club addressed by Mr. Bazeley, Mr. Freak and Mr. James Gribble from Northampton, who was the Union's permanent organiser and later strike manager. Resolutions demanding full statement prices were carried enthusiastically. Members, who went on strike, were promised fifteen shillings per week Union benefit with an additional five shillings from Federation funds, which would be more than many were getting from regular employment.

Before the first of March, 1905, the employers were told that as from that date the employees would claim the prices as agreed. No acceptable answer being received, an official strike was called, and began to take effect from the third of March.

[14] The 'Rushden Echo', a local newspaper commented :-

"It is exceedingly regrettable that the contractors should have repudiated the statement of prices to which in conjunction with representatives of the workmen, they recently agreed. Under the circumstances the workmen had no alternative but to go out on strike to force the contractors to pay the statement wages, and in their struggle they have practically the whole of the people with them - - - - it is safe to predict that the ultimate victory will be with the men."

THE STRIKE

As the reader is now aware, the local press reported the troubles in considerable detail and, as a consequence, the national newspapers were soon on the scene. Not all their reports were complimentary, however, as in the following extract from the Manchester Guardian of 23rd March, 1905, commenting on the rural nature of the environs of Raunds and, by inference, doubting whether any good could come out of the dispute :-

"You must walk a mile from the [local railway station]. . . before you see anything more than the church steeple and the windmill sails of the town, and nearly another mile before you come to the houses and boot factories. The buildings are widely scattered, to call so rural a place a town is purely complimentary. Cows stare over the fence on one side of the main street, and crows come foraging in the market place. . . ."[15]

By the time the above piece had appeared in print, the strike had entered its third week. During the first week, from those firms which refused to pay the settlement prices, 300 to 400 came out or gave a week's notice, and these premises were picketed. The firms involved were listed in local papers as :- "J Kingsmith & Son, Adams Bros., O. Smith & Co., Clarke & Haynes, J.T.Tebbutt & Co., C. Nichols & Co., The Crispin Productive Societies, Phillips & Co., The Wellington Boot Co., Mr. R. Coggins, Mr. W. Lawrence."[16] One contractor, John Kingsmith & Son was interviewed and agreed to pay, so the men were ordered in accordingly, although it was stated, by other contractors, that none of the contracts around which the dispute centred were involved. At a meeting of employers it was declared impossible to concede to the demands of the workmen.[17]

In Ringstead, Adams Bros. (mentioned above) owned a small branch factory employing 32 men but were unable to persuade them to continue working during the strike. As a consequence, an attempt was made to open another factory in Kettering but only two men turned up to work.[17a] By March 17th, some 500 men were on strike so that mass meetings had to be held in the open air. One such meeting on Monday, March 13th, assembled on Nichols Hill, which no longer exists but was apparently at the junction of Brook Street, Grove Street and Thorpe Street. Here it was announced that several factories had been forced to close down completely.

An excellent organiser, James Gribble, was a bundle of energy, calling meeting after meeting to urge the strikers to stand firm. He had served in the regular army and risen to the rank of Quartermaster Sergeant before returning to civilian life in Northampton. His ability to get things done was only matched by his fiery nature as subsequent events were to show. At a meeting of nearly 200 women closers, he pointed out that because Raunds was different from other centres in that the army boots were closed by hand, if they stood shoulder to shoulder with the men, the manufacturers would be defeated. He suggested to the men, at a meeting on the Square, they should not pay rents (usually four shillings per week) to any manufacturers who happened to own the houses in which they lived.

It would seem that approximately two thirds of the labour force were on strike although no exact figures are available. From the start, some non-unionists had crossed the picket lines to fetch work out, and one cannot but have sympathy with them particularly in view of the fact that the strikers were receiving up to £1 per week in strike pay. The plight of their families is illustrated by the following short item appearing in a Northampton newspaper :-

[18] *"Church Parade. Beautiful weather favoured the church parade on Sunday last in aid of the women and children of the non-unionist workers now out on strike. The parade started from the Red Lion headed by the Raunds Temperance Band and proceeded to the church. Favoured by the bright and welcome sunshine crowds of people lined the streets along the route of the procession. A bright and hearty service was held in the church and an excellent address was given by the Vicar (the Rev. E.E. Law) on 'Labour' with especial reference to the strike now pending.*

Collection: £5-10s-11d

A collection at the evening service at the Primitive Methodist Chapel realised: £1-2s-2d"

A further report announced that the Raunds Temperance Band was planning to tour the county to raise money for the non-unionist families.[19]

If there was a good deal of sympathy extended to the dependants of non-unionists, this goodwill did not include the menfolk. From the outset, strike breakers were followed home, hooted at, and threatened with tin cans and rotten eggs. Some stone throwing was reported on Tuesday, March 21st, but on the following day a crowd of 500 or 600 people, including children, followed the 'Blacklegs' and 'Traitors' home, beating tin kettles, and becoming increasingly hostile. Someone picked up a stone and threw it at a non-unionist's house window. In no time, the whole crowd joined in so that every pane of glass was quickly smashed. Thus began a night of violence until nearly every non-unionist's house had been attacked. There were only two members of the constabulary available and they were powerless to disperse the rioters until 10 p.m. Local and national papers carried headlines such as, "RAUNDS RIOTS" with increased coverage of the dispute running, in some cases, to six columns of newsprint.[20]

The next day thirty extra police officers were drafted in to impose some order. But even they could not prevent an attack on the house of Mr. Groome who was the Manager of the St. Crispins Productive Society situated in Sackville Street. The London newspapers made the most of the disturbances, in their usual sensationalist way, even printing photographs of houses which had been partially demolished before the strike, as examples of damage caused by the riots. It has to be admitted, however, that some manufacturers' residences had been attacked and some factory windows broken.

The prosecution of a number of rowdy elements led to the imposition of fines by the local magistrates sitting at Thrapston Police Court. At least one of those fined refused to pay and elected to go to prison,[21] but the prompt action by the authorities brought things, more or less, under control. The Trade Union paid for the defence of Union members brought before the Court which action was certainly appreciated by all concerned and not least by the organiser, James Gribble.

During the first few weeks of the dispute, attempts were made by various Members of Parliament to bring the causes of the workers' distress to the attention of Mr. Arnold Forster, the Secretary of State for War in Arthur Balfour's Conservative administration. Mr. Channing, the Liberal M.P. for Peterborough, in which constituency Raunds was then situated, asked whether the Secretary of State was aware that the statement of wages, agreed upon and accepted by the War Office, had been set aside by several contractors. Mr. Forster replied in the usual obfuscating manner, beloved of politicians, to the effect that when the Department had reason to believe the wage clause was being infringed, steps would be taken to secure its observance. Which, of course, went against all the evidence so patently provided by the Raunds controversy. Clearly, it would take some outstanding event, or action, to move the Minister from his intransigent position.

Towards the end of April, several manufacturers stated that they would open their factories at the old terms, but only two girls went in for a short time. So, the strike continued until the ninth week when about 300 went back at the old rates of pay.[22]   It seemed that the employers had won their case as in the much larger stoppages of 1894 and 1897!

Councillor James Gribble

However, this was not to be the outcome, Councillor James Gribble had other ideas. Perhaps he had been reading about the protests of the Russian people, in January 1905, when they marched to the Czar's palace in St. Petersburg, but his proposals were extraordinary. He suggested nothing less than a march to London to present the men's grievances to the War Office and the Secretary of State in person. If this failed, they would proceed to Windsor and present their just demands to King Edward VII when he returned from Paris.

The Trade Union officials disapproved of the whole scheme and thought it could only end in disaster bringing discredit to their cause. They refused to back their own organiser and tried to dissuade him; so that when the strike was over he promptly resigned from his position. In the minutes of the Rushden Branch of the N.U.B.S.O. the strike is fully recorded but with no mention of the march. A history of the Union published in 1924 does not mention the march although it is given good coverage in Alan Fox's History of the Union (1874 – 1957) published in 1958.

THE MARCH TO LONDON

Once the plan was announced, there was no shortage of volunteers to join the great adventure. Over 300 men presented themselves before 'General' Gribble who selected 115 representatives as being those likely to make the journey without undue discomfort. The outward stage of seventy miles would be via Rushden, Bedford, Luton, Harpenden, St. Albans, Watford, Cricklewood to London (Hyde Park). It would be twenty miles further on the return leg through Chesham, Leighton Buzzard, Newport Pagnell, Northampton, Wellingborough and Rushden.

Before commencement, on Monday May 8th, Gribble revised his strategy   thus :-

[23]*"We shall go to the War Office and present a petition, pleading with the authorities to interfere and insist on manufacturers recognising the Fair Wages Clause in contracts. Failing satisfaction there, we shall march to Westminster and present a petition to be heard at the Bar of the House of Commons. I know we shall be turned back, but the public will learn the justice of our demands. We shall not go to Windsor because that would be useless, but we shall take other steps to acquaint the King of the*

reality of our grievance."

The thoroughness of the preparations for the undertaking was quite remarkable. The little 'army' was formed on military lines using all Gribble's experience as a regular soldier. There would be three officers under the General's command, whose duties were designated as Paymaster, Billetmaster, and Commissariat General. (From where did he get that name?) Three men formed a Cycle Corps whose duties involved riding ahead to make arrangements in the next town. One solitary man was to be the Ambulance providing First Aid. The rest of the men were divided into five companies each commanded by a Sergeant, while a sixth company of eleven formed a brass band under command of a bandmaster.

On Sunday evening of May 7th the men were drilled on a piece of land belonging to the Woodbine Club. A bugle was used to muster the marchers and the drilling was strictly regimental, in ranks of four, as was the custom in the British army at that time.

The march leaving Raunds on Monday 8th May 1905

Part 4: THE MARCH TO LONDON

Monday morning began at 8.15 a.m. with a meeting in the Woodbine Club followed by assembly on the Square in their companies. The band struck up the lively march 'Rebecca' as the

John (Crutchy) Pearson, the crippled
Ringstead bootmaker with three other marchers

men, with haversacks and coats neatly rolled up on their backs, strode proudly down Brook Street to the cheers of men, women and children. The selected party were followed by a few not chosen, but determined to make the journey anyway, and included John Pearson from Ringstead who went all the way on crutches.

The whole proceedings were noted by representatives of the local and national press together with photographers and even cinematograph operators. Not all the newspapers were full of praise for the venture as is apparent in the following extract from the weekly 'Northampton Mercury'. The reporter wrote :-

[24]*"I could not help contrasting two incidents. When the agricultural labourers, with Joseph Arch as their leader, determined to process the country (in 1874) they had few to champion their cause, and there was nothing of theatrical display about their procedure. They came into Northampton, I well remember, a grim looking, determined lot of men whom many people looked down upon as a lot of 'agitators' and who were deserving of little sympathy in the methods they were adopting. Northampton, to its credit, gave the men a rousing welcome.*

In those days, of course, there was not a shoal of London newspapers on the look out for, or ready to make, sensational copy, and perhaps the fact that such exist today accounts for the different feeling I experienced on Monday when I saw the Raunds men start upon their 70 mile journey to 'town'. I could not, somehow, get rid of the impression, that whatever may be the motive of the journey, the fact it was to be undertaken had been utilised too much as a newspaper sensation.

In saying this I do not for one minute wish to discredit the good intentions of those who initiated or who are taking part in the march.

But the little crowd of London journalists, the myriad cameras focussed on the scene, the cinematograph operators, securing pictures for public display, and the whole 'tone' of the procedure, seemed to mark the thing as a bit overdone." (What would he have written today?)

Despite these adverse comments, the fact that the enterprise was to be undertaken, stirred the nation as much for the imagination and boldness of the plan, as for the execution of it. The thoroughness of the organisation was demonstrated again by the card which every member of the party carried containing the following endorsement :-

"RAUNDS STRIKERS' MARCH TO LONDON

This is to certify that _____ _____, No. ____, is a member of the deputation marching from Raunds to lay a memorial before Mr. Arnold Forster.

(signed) James Gribble"

The first morning's route through Stanwick to Higham Ferrers
An illustration from The Sphere - 'an illustrated newspaper for the home'

Part 4: THE MARCH TO LONDON

The first morning's route through Stanwick to Higham Ferrers, preceded by four police constables led by police sergeant Cameron, was graphically described by the Kettering 'Evening Telegraph' reporter, who accompanied the marchers and sent in his impressions at each stage :-

[25] *"After leaving Raunds we were accompanied by shopmates and others as far as Stanwick. Here we were met by more than half the population of the village. 'What oh!' called out one woman, 'Aint we 'aving a time.' Mr. Gribble marched by my side, and if ever there looked a man who could march it is Mr. Gribble. His stout, thick-set figure looked when marching as if it were wound up, and as if not even the War Office would stop him. Several women with perambulators came from Raunds as far as Stanwick with us, much to the mystifying of the children, who wondered where daddy was going with a parcel on his back. On entering Stanwick we were greeted by large crowds, and as we marched through were accorded a real Stanwick reception. Though we all started with black boots, even by this time they were thickly covered with dust (No universal tarmac on roads in 1905). 'GENERAL' Gribble- as he was quickly dubbed- called us to attention on entering the village, for on the way the ranks had become rather ragged. No smoking is allowed through villages, the sergeants seeing that all pipes are put out. By the time we left Stanwick I was able to get along much easier, for no perambulators or mailcarts now took up the part of the road left free by the strikers. The marchers quickly spotted me, and gave the TELEGRAPH representative, who is to do the march with them to London, a warm welcome.*

"If we're not working for boot manufacturers we're making money for you", was their opinion.

From Stanwick to Higham was a steady march without music from the band, but to the whistled accompaniment of 'John Brown's body'. By this time the excitement of the starting had worn off, and the tramp, tramp, tramp was about all that could be heard. Whenever a trap or cart passed, the collectors always made it a point to try for a contribution, and generally they got it too. Just before the top of the hill into Higham was reached the ranks were reformed and the march taken up with something like precision."

Higham was traversed without a pause with the band playing the march 'Edwinston'. Then on to Rushden along a crowded street, stopping briefly outside the Trade Union headquarters in Higham Road where Mr. Warren East was observed with his

The strikers arriving at Rushden, where each man had a meal of bread and cheese.
Here the strikers were heartily welcomed, and many were offered more substantial
refreshment than they carried for themselves.
(Perhaps this is Higham Ferrers - Author)

Part 4: THE MARCH TO LONDON

The march between Rushden and Bedford near the junction of Park Lane, Sharnbrook.
The band played 'Rule Britannia' when they entered a town. J. Bass, G. Sawford and C. Mayes the cyclists, rode ahead
to arrange food and overnight accommodation.

cinematograph capturing the moment for posterity. A halt was made for lunch at the Green opposite the parish church of St. Mary. Then after refreshments, the marchers and a large crowd of onlookers and supporters were addressed by Mr. Charles Bates, the president of the local branch of the Union. The meeting began with the singing of a Trade Union hymn, 'O ye moiling, toiling masses', sung to the tune of 'Men of Harlech'.

Rushden was left at 1.40 p.m. with a small crowd following and the marchers in fine voice with songs such as, 'Dolly Gray' and 'The Church's One Foundation'. [26]A stop was made at The Falcon at Bletsoe, where beer was served from buckets supplied by

Marching from Raunds to Bedford. Councillor Gribble marked with a cross.

Messrs. Nunneley, Meadows and Knight of Raunds (Publicans?), and food laden tables provided.

The march towards Bedford continued apace so that the town was reached at 6 p.m. and the men dismissed at Howard's statue with warnings to behave in a fitting manner. Later, 500 people attended a meeting on the Market Square where Mr. Gribble explained what all the fuss was about and was greeted with rounds of applause. Every member of the party found accommodation for the night, so that an early start was able to be made on Tuesday morning after the bugler called them together. The first day's collection had totalled £10-1s-5d.

Before the next stage commenced, the E.T. Reporter spoke to Mr. Thody, Chief Constable, who said there had been no complaints about the conduct of the strikers who behaved with dignity and decorum throughout. By 8.30 a.m. the marchers reassembled in Silver Street being given a hearty send off [27] as they departed for Luton, while the band played 'The bright smile haunts me still'. Not one man had dropped out!

At Clophill, south of Bedford, a rest was taken by mistake, as they were scheduled to stop at Silsoe. But error or not,

The Army bootmakers marching from Bedford yesterday. Councillor James Gribble, their leader, walking by the side of the column, is indicated by a cross.

photographs taken at the scene by the side of the River Ivel, show the men partaking refreshments, and soaking their feet in the cool water. A surprising number of local inhabitants found time to survey the unusual sight considering it was not a holiday.

Part 1: INTRODUCTION

On the way to Clophill a lady, living in a cottage beside the road, offered to loan the strikers a pony and trap, while a farmer's wife offered a horse and cart. However, all offers of lifts were

The marchers resting at Clophill

refused although pennies were accepted as contributions. Many sympathisers gave small amounts of money to the marchers and a gentleman in a motor-car handed over a gold sovereign to swell the funds.

As the weary band trudged up hill towards Barton, a country milk cart carrying something draped in black was passed with six sorrowing mourners following behind. *"Hats off"*, was the command of Councillor Gribble as the men marched past[28]. Later in the afternoon, while a rest was being taken at the top of Barton Cutting, the Chief Constable of Luton arrived to meet and inspect this contingent of striking boot-makers determined, it must be

A rest being taken at Barton Cutting

Crowds of people welcoming the marchers to Luton

Part 4: THE MARCH TO LONDON

assumed, not to allow a rabble to enter Luton. He was very impressed by the smartness of their drill, and the entry into the town resembled the triumphal march of a successful army.

The E.T. reporter wrote[29]:- *"Halting at the Liberal Club we disbanded and after a wash, sat down in the assembly room, to a*

A welcome wash and shave at Luton Liberal Club

The collectors taking in money to keep the marching bootmakers in food and lodging.
Sympathy was expressed substantially, the good behaviour of the men earning commendation.

meat tea provided by the Deputy Mayor, Mr. A. Oakley and his brother Alderman Oakley. The Deputy Mayor announced that what he did for labour was only what he owed to labour. Every marcher was then handed a cigar and a barber offered to shave all 115 free of charge! After the glorious tea, votes of thanks were the order of the day and heartily endorsed."

Two thousand people were present, later that evening, to hear speeches from 'General' Gribble and local Trade Union leaders. As in Bedford everyone was found comfortable accommodation for the night. In fact the beds were so homely and restful that the party did not assemble to leave for St. Albans until 11.30 a.m. Prior to this the men were told of a despicable fraud which had taken place at Elstow on Tuesday morning. Apparently two men posing as Raunds strikers had been collecting money from cottagers on their own account.

Another reason for delay was caused by Mr. Gribble sending a letter to the Secretary of State for War asking that the deputation be received. He also sent a message to the Conservative Prime Minister, the Rt. Hon. A.J. Balfour, asking him to use his influence to induce Mr. Forster to meet them. The response to these requests was a peremptory refusal to meet or discuss the men's grievances.

On the third day of the march, £7-10s-2d was collected from well-wishers as they travelled through Harpenden to St. Albans. This was a departure from an earlier plan to visit Dunstable. Harpenden was reached at 12.30 p.m. and the intrepid E.T. reporter wrote :-

[30] *"Weather hot, roads very dusty. Mr. Gribble maintains the strictest discipline all through, his, 'Left, left, left!' being heard*

Councillor James Gribble, the leader of the strikers, eating a frugal lunch. It is to his credit and that of the men he leads that not a single case of disorderly behavior has been recorded during the march.

Part 4: THE MARCH TO LONDON

"General" Gribbles's band halted for refreshments supplied to them by the sympathising bootmakers of Harpenden, who turned out to wish their friends "God speed" on their march to London.

throughout the day. Everybody is covered with dust, but no one is complaining of 'feet' this morning and every man who started has reached Harpenden."

Here, at what was then only a village according to a Northampton newspaper reporter :-

[31] *"On the village green a delightful picnic had been prepared. Spread out beneath the shade a lunch was waiting. The scene was a most charming and picturesque one, and in such good spirits were the men that after the feast some of them danced on the green with village maidens who had waited at table. The break at this delightful spot lasted until three thirty, again after votes of thanks, cheers and tunes from the band, the tramp was renewed . . . ."*

What the wives and girlfriends thought about this report is not recorded. Particularly as the E.T. reporter wrote only that, *"Many marchers fell fast asleep in the shade, but two or three may have gone for a walk – just for exercise!"*

Part 4: THE MARCH TO LONDON

John Pearson

Perhaps the Northampton man was exaggerating, but in any event St. Albans was reached at 6 p.m. where the deputation from Raunds was met by the usual crowds as well as trade union representatives. The Liberal Club gave them a meal paid for by the St. Albans Trade Council and fifty local workmen provided beds for the night. Before everyone bedded down, however, the usual evening meeting was held in the Town Square. As well as 'General' Gribble, the crowd heard from Mr. T. O'Grady, Secretary of the London branch of the N.U.B.S.O. and members of the London Trades Council. The Liberal agent praised the turn out of the marchers and it was announced that Wednesday's collection now amounted to £20-2s-3d.

A progressive councillor supplied breakfast, again at the Liberal Club and also the Clarendon Hotel. Everyone had been

Men on the journey to the War Office writing home to tell their families how they were getting on.
Many carried writing materials and sent long accounts of each day's events to their wives in Northamptonshire.

found a bed for the night but it was generally agreed not as comfortable as at Luton. One man said, *"Except we slept with King Teddy himself, we couldn't beat Luton."* Someone bought a pound of boracic powder and distributed it to sprinkle in the socks of the marchers. A marcher remarked that he could not see his feet for blisters, yet a few made up a party and went to look over the ancient Abbey. There was great anxiety among the men to be taken in some photographs and get their faces in the paper.

Before the marchers left for Watford on the next stage of their trek, several councillors praised the fitness of the men. The E.T. reporter phoned back to his paper in the following terms at 11.15 a.m.

[32] *"Mr. Benthal, a St. Albans' worthy said he had seldom seen a finer lot of men. 'Nor better looking,' a voice called out —. Just resuming our march. J. Pearson, the cripple, is marching in front*

James Gravestock, an ancient labourer, singing to the strikers at Garston. His song consisted of fifty verses, of which the marchers could only listen to only thirty-three, as they had to hurry southwards in the direction of Mr Arnold Forster.

to keep out of the dust."

"OFFICIAL ARRANGEMENTS FOR FRIDAY MAY 12TH
    6 a.m.   leave Watford
    11 a.m. refreshments at Crown Hotel, Cricklewood
    1 p.m.   dinner at Eyre Arms, St John's Wood
    7 p.m.   proprietors of Reynolds News provide supper
((On Sunday the Marylebone S.D.F. (Social Democratic Federation) are providing dinner.))"

On the road towards Garston the strikers passed several boot factories and a detachment of Yeomanry (Volunteer Cavalry), but whether the horse soldiers had been deliberately deployed or were

Group shot in Watford.

merely on exercise is not made clear. The military men gave the marchers loud cheers as they passed and donated a good deal of money to the funds.

Watford was reached at about 5.30 p.m., with the men in the best of spirits, as they may well have been, having eaten dinner at, The Three Horseshoes Public House, Garston[33]. The meal was served in the meadow where copies of the Kettering Evening Telegraph were distributed among the men which they read with their socks off, bathing their feet in the solutions of boracic powder.

A deputation of the local Trades and Labour Council met the marchers on the outskirts of the town and marched with them behind the band. Great crowds followed this procession to the Watford Labour Church, where a tea was provided by the veteran Social Democratic politician, J.E. Williams. Hundreds of people wanted to know where Pearson the cripple was to be found, as his bravery in keeping up while using crutches was by now well known.

The usual mass meeting in Watford Market Place was marked by 'General' Gribble announcing that he had received a letter from Mr. Arnold Forster stating that the Government had granted an inquiry into the dispute, but that no-one would receive a deputation. Despite this rebuff the march must continue as Mr. Channing, the Liberal M.P. for East Northamptonshire, had certainly agreed to receive them.

As on the previous three nights, beds were found either at, or through, the local Labour Church. Reveille on Friday morning was 5 a.m. and breakfast was arranged for the men at The Lime Tree Restaurant,[33a] paid for by Messrs. Blyth and Pratt, blacking manufacturers. At 6.30 a.m. the marchers set off for Bushey on the way to Cricklewood and London. The E.T. reporter commented :-
[34] *"Very little rain has fallen since we left Raunds which makes the roads very dusty. Police Superintendent Harlan has followed us from Luton. 'A better lot of travellers I've never seen', he said. 'I've heard no complaints from anyone and I'm surprised at the little bad language I've heard.' The collection in Watford amounted to £24-19s-2d."*

At 7 a.m. the dusty party reached Bushey, but not one man had fallen out. Here it was announced that a plan had been formed to march down Oxford Street through Trafalgar Square and Whitehall to Westminster. Unfortunately, the Metropolitan Police were not in favour and, in the event, this plan had to be abandoned.

The photograph on the left shows the Raunds men marching through Kilburn after their eighty mile journey to lay their grievances before the War Office. On the right they are lunching at the Crown Hotel, Cricklewood. They were enthusiastically received in North London.

The good news was that lodgings would be found at Carrington House, a London County Council hostel at Deptford, free of charge.

The route now lay through Stanmore and Edgware to Hendon. All along the way roads were crowded with curious sightseers who had been anxiously waiting to see the, by now famous, marchers for hours. When Hendon was reached at 11 a.m. refreshments were made available courtesy of The Railway Servants' Union. The rest was very welcome as the E.T. reporter noted that John Pearson the cripple, was getting very tired.

The next halt, at 12.30 p.m., was at the Crown Inn, Cricklewood where another capital feed was provided by the proprietor of the hotel, Mr. G. Hollam. A rousing speech, in praise of the men of Raunds and their mission, was made by Mr. Harry Quelch, secretary of the local Trades Council. A further £20 was donated to the funds through the generosity of the Council. It was during this break in the march that 'General' Gribble advised the men to drink no intoxicating beverages and added that if they were to be feted every mile or two, their next feed should be "Beecham's!" [35] (Beecham's Liver Pills – a remedy for upset stomachs.)

Gribble's words were prophetic as at the subsequent stop at St. John's Wood (near Lord's cricket ground) another good square feed was produced by Mr. Rutherford, a local tradesman. The meal was followed by a music hall type concert which featured

The visiting bootmakers were enthusiastically received when they marched into Hyde Park yesterday afternoon. They were welcomed with music and flags. The people appeared to think their efforts to influence the War Office would succeed.

Part 4: THE MARCH TO LONDON

Fred Templar, a comedian and other artists. The Londoners, it seemed, had already taken the bootmaking strikers from Raunds to their hearts. When the march restarted at 3 p.m., it was discovered that the 'General', who looked exhausted and was himself feeling unwell, had handed over control to the Social Democratic Federation. The organisation during the stay in London would be in the hands of the S.D.F., but Gribble would not desert his troops and expressed his determination to see the job completed.

The E.T. reporter:

[36]*"I had a run down to Marble Arch (by bicycle) and found a crowd of between 8,000 and 10,000 people eagerly awaiting the arrival of the marchers. I also spoke to some police officers who said they had no instructions to stop the procession. They had heard such good accounts, that the Raunds' men would probably be allowed to march all the way."*

Alas, such optimism was not well founded, and the meeting in Hyde Park was as far as the 115 would be allowed to process, for the time being. At around 3.45 p.m., the marchers entered Hyde Park by Marble Arch accompanied by 200 London Trade Unionists, and preceded by mounted policemen, who were needed to force a way through the crowds, to the meeting point where a platform had been erected. Several Labour leaders and London Trades Council members addressed the cheering supporters.

It may well be supposed that the police had been surprised by the number of enthusiastic well wishers, who were assembled not only in the park but also in Trafalgar Square, along Whitehall, and in Parliament Square. Only a small deputation of 10 was permitted to continue to the House of Commons, preceded by Councillor Gribble with one companion, in a cab. The small group of strikers were escorted by police and cheered all the way, although the

This represents the deputation of the strikers who set out for the House of Commons on the arrival of their little army. The police would not allow the main body within a mile of the House.

throng waiting in Trafalgar Square were bitterly disappointed at not being able to applaud the main body of marchers who were taken to Deptford in a number of brakes. (Brake – a large wagonette or horse bus.)

In the lobby of the House of Commons 'General' Gribble and

his depleted army were met by Mr. David James Shackleton,[37] M.P. for Clitheroe and chairman of the national Labour Party, and conducted to Conference Room Number 1 where a number of other M.P.s were waiting including Mr. F.A. Channing, Member for East Northamptonshire; Mr. Will. Crooks, Member for Woolwich (first Labour Mayor in London); Mr Keir Hardie, Member for Merthyr (father of the Labour Party); Mr. Arthur Henderson, Member for Barnard Castle, (prominent Labour leader and statesman) together with Mr. Field and Mr. Nannetti. A friendly discussion took place during which time messages were sent to Mr. Arnold Forster, the Secretary of State for War, and to Mr. Bromley Davenport, the Financial Secretary to the War Office, to inform them that the deputation from Raunds had arrived, but neither of the two gentlemen could be found!

The deputation was then taken to the Strangers' Gallery in the House of Commons. What happened next is best described in Gribble's own words:

[38] *"This was exceedingly annoying (the fact that Mr. Arnold Forster refused to meet them) - - - - and I was determined that we should not go back without something happening. I had an order for the Stranger's Gallery and I went there. I heard members talking and talking (the debate was about Women's Suffrage), and I wondered if this sort of thing was going to last for ever. So I decided to take some action, and I rose and asked (shouted out) if this gentleman was going to talk the House out. I informed the House that I had brought 115 men from Raunds in Northamptonshire to see Mr. Arnold Forster - - - - that they had marched all that distance in order to lay their grievances before the House, but now I found that nothing was likely to be done. I had just got to that point when several . . . . attendants . . . . caught hold of me, and I was turned*

out. But I was determined not to give in without another effort, so I made a run for the Inner Lobby (leading to the Commons chamber). I did not, however, get very far. Other officials of the House caught me, and prevented me getting anywhere near the Bar. Then the Sergeant-at-Arms ordered me to be removed from the building, and I was removed . . . . "

A number of ladies, who were waiting for the result of the Suffrage debate, were in the lobby while the 'General' was being arrested and called out, *"What a shame!"* and *"Treat him gently!"* Every part of this incident was observed by the lobby correspondents of the national newspapers and was flamboyantly headlined in the next day's editions. All of which was, without doubt, exactly the sort of publicity the 'little man in the red tie', as some papers described him, had aimed for.

In fact, negotiations on behalf of the strikers had been initiated by four M.P.s with Mr. Arnold Forster, after a debate on army clothing estimates in April. 'The Times'[39] newspaper reported, on the day after the marchers left Raunds, that negotiations were well advanced and two days later printed the following:-

[40] *"It having been suggested to the Secretary of State for War that action should be taken under the Fair Wage Resolution in reference to certain War Office contracts for army boots, he had determined to cause an immediate and special inquiry to be made - - -."*

Very soon after the dramatic scenes in the House of Commons the War Office announced that a distinguished lawyer, Mr. G.R.Askwith was to head the inquiry to investigate wages in the army boot trade. With this already underway, or at least prepared, the Minister of State saw no reason to grant an interview with the deputation from Raunds. Indeed, no government ministry likes to be seen to be acting under duress or giving in to intimidation. All this may have been the government's impression of the situation, but the striking bootmakers were certain they had won their case. The next two days were in the nature of a holiday for the 115 marchers. Indeed, the whole fortnight was described as the best time of his life, by one of the marchers interviewed by a local reporter in 1937. [41]*"It was beautiful weather throughout,"* he remembered. While in London their meals were catered for in the Church Army's 'King's Labour Tents', near the Strand. The provisioning being in the hands of Captain Sim of the 'Morning Post's' Thames Embankment Labour Home but also supported by 'Reynolds News'. On the Sunday afternoon, the Rev. W. Carlile, honorary chief secretary of the Church Army, invited the strikers to tea after 5 p.m. followed by a religious service at Whitefield's Tabernacle in Tottenham Court Road. The evening concluded with lantern and cinematograph views. On the Monday morning the men were entertained to breakfast by the Committee of the National Liberal Club.

Between times, on the previous Friday evening, the marchers were right royally amused and delighted by being invited to the Lyceum Music Hall where John Pearson, the cripple, showed off his prowess on the stage, and was presented with a pair of spring-loaded crutches. The London Trades Council had voted money for entertainment, and on Saturday the Royal Italian Circus gave a free show for the Raunds strikers.

However, the stay in the capital was not entirely a relaxation as the S.D.F. were determined to utilise the occasion to boost their 'Right to Work' campaign. [42]On Sunday afternoon, at 2.30, the 115 bootmaker strikers assembled under the Charing Cross railway arch and were joined by contingents of Socialist and Labour

"General" Gribble, leader of the Raunds strikers, who was ejected from the House of Commons on May 12, made a stirring speech on behalf of the strikers in Trafalgar Square on Sunday.

organisations. A procession was formed, and headed by a brass band playing the 'Marseillaise', they marched into Trafalgar Square with banners unfurled. A crowd of fully 10,000 people cheered them in, and it was obvious from the variety of banners that most metropolitan labour groups were represented. The emblems of the Union of Boot and Shoe Operatives, together with those of the Army Clothing Department Employees Union, were

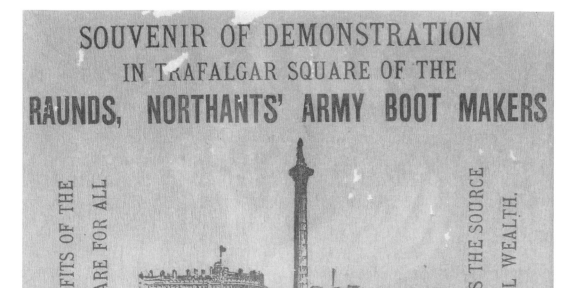

Rare souvenir handkerchief produced for the Trafalgar Square demonstration.

Part 4: THE MARCH TO LONDON

displayed on the plinth which was used as a speakers' platform. The largest crowd seen on the Square for a number of years threw coins onto the plinth, for the benefit of the men from Raunds, as they waited for the speeches to begin.

There were three platforms set up presided over by Mr. S. Michaels, president of the Cabdrivers' Union, Mr. J. Green, of the Social Democratic Federation, and Mr. W. Thorne, of the Gasworkers' Union. The main speaker, however, was Mr. Keir Hardie M.P. who spoke from two sides of the plinth. This is what he had to say:-

[43] *"I know of few events in the Labour movement which have been more effective than the one the success of which we are celebrating. Instead of condemning I am inclined to bless Mr. Arnold Forster. Had he listened at first to the demands of the men, the march from Raunds would never have taken place, and the workers of England would have been left to stew in their stupidity under the belief that all was going well with them. But the evil of which they complained rested not with Mr. Arnold Forster nor with the Government. Governments do not elect themselves; they are what the working men of England make them. If the workers would do a little more for themselves at the ballot box they would not be required to do so much in Trafalgar Square. - - - - - - If they want their wrongs redressed, if they want the Government to set an example to employers of labour, they must do in London what was being done throughout the provinces – organise the Socialist and Trade Union forces and send Labour members to the House of Commons."[44] (Cheers)*

Mr J. Gribble, the organiser of the Raunds marchers, said the work undertaken a week ago was effective, and it had been worth working for. The strikers had called the attention of the country to the anomalies that existed under the so-called fair wages clause, and he believed the march would be the means of introducing a clause for the payment of trade union rates of wages in all Army contracts in the future. They had demonstrated that labour, if properly organised, would intimidate even a Tory Government. Mr. Arnold Forster would not grant an inquiry into the question of the prices that were being paid in the Raunds district by certain contractors, although the men approached him on several occasions. However, after the organised workers had been four days on the march to London, he promised to hold an immediate inquiry into the question. - - - - (Cheers)

There followed other speeches by various trade union leaders,

The expenses were met by collecting en route, and the party received a most enthusiastic reception at all stopping places.

Part 4: THE MARCH TO LONDON

including one from Mrs. Despard, the veteran suffragette. Several resolutions in support of the strikers were put to the rally and passed unanimously, with many more cheers and pledges of support, before the crowd dispersed just after 5 p.m.

THE RETURN TO RAUNDS

At 10 a.m. on Monday morning the strikers' supporters gathered at Marble Arch in preparation for the march homeward. Most of the Raunds men were not sorry to get away from London. Some of the marchers when questioned gave revealing replies :-

[45] *"Ah, I've learnt more in the last two days than I've ever done before in my life," was a general comment. "It's a fine place" was all that someone else would say about London. "Well," said another, "I always said I'd never come to London unless I walked there, and I'm blessed if it ain't come true."*

After the breakfast provided by the National Liberal Club, Mr. Gribble was presented with a cheque for £50 on behalf of the proprietors of the 'Daily News'. Whether the money was a thank you to the marchers for all the copy they had supplied, or a genuine token of support is not known. However, this was only one of a number of donations made to the strikers before they departed.

Marching in fine style the little army entered Hyde Park where a crowd of 7,000 was assembled. Short speeches were again made by Mr. Gribble, Mr Keir Hardie, and Mrs. Despard (incidentally the sister of General French), the Rev. D. Pughe and Mr. J. Williams. The last named declared the strikers' march to London to be the greatest movement for labour since the dock strike of 1887. The 'General' then called the men to attention and the order

Mr. E. Bird, the oldest of the marching strikers. In six months he will be sixty.

to 'march' was given as the band struck up a rousing tune and led the way north towards the Edgware Road. A large contingent of police was needed to force a way through the cheering crowds of thousands of people gathered to give them a tremendous send off. *"The Edgware Road was thronged on each side almost all the way to Kilburn.."[46]* The departure time had been delayed until 11 a.m., but a steady march took them as far as Cricklewood which was

Part 5: THE RETURN TO RAUNDS

reached one hour later. Having sprained his ankle a few days earlier, Mr. Gribble was forced to ride in a wagonette, although John Pearson started gamely and was determined to walk at least as far as Watford.

At the Crown Inn, a previous watering hole, all the men were photographed in groups and a local tobacconist gave each marcher a portion of American Blend tobacco. After the rest, the party continued to Edgware for lunch. Cash collections were taken along the way with large amounts being contributed. The Congregational minister at Edgware made his chapel rooms available for rest and refreshment, and then it became a hard slog towards Watford traversing very hilly roads. No long stops were made at Stanmore or Bushey, despite the crowds of cheering supporters, so that Watford was reached at about 6.30 p.m. Not so many people appeared on the streets as on the previous Thursday, but everyone was accommodated at the same locations as before. After tea and refreshments, Mr Gribble was presented with an address by the members of the Watford Labour Church, Watford Trades Council, Watford I.L.P., Callow Socialist and Labour Representation Committee and the Watford Labour League. After a long preamble it concluded :-

[47]*"We wish to place on record our testimony to the splendid and irreproachable conduct of the strikers whilst they were among us, and to express our admiration for their leader, Councillor Gribble, who by his courage, discipline, and good judgment, has done much to ensure for his men and their just cause the sympathy and support of the great mass of the people.*

In conclusion, we confidently express the hope that the Government will be forced by public opinion to insist that the claims of the bootmakers of Raunds shall be fully met; and that at

Part 5: THE RETURN TO RAUNDS

the next General Election such a proportion of Socialist and Labour candidates will be returned to Parliament as to ensure full consideration to the claims of Labour without the necessity of a march to London to represent these to the Government."

A concert party then entertained the whole assembly at the Liberal Club, which was much appreciated. Later, the usual assembly in the town square was regaled with more socialist and trade union exhortations until, tired but happy, the strikers and supporters retired to bed.

After the excitement of leaving London, the next stage of the march to Chesham, was not commenced until noon. A crowd of 700 saw the men on their way, but not until Labour songs had been sung including, 'The Old Red Flag'. 'General' Gribble decided to follow in a trap which proved a useful deposit for the men's discarded coats as the weather continued to be warm and sunny. Pearson elected to once again lead the way although his brand new spring-loaded crutches were also left in the trap.

All the men were glad to see the countryside and breathe fresh air again. The smoke of the Metropolitan Railway had been exceptionally distasteful, and the fragrance and quiet of the country, after the smell of hot melting tar, and the rush of London, seemed like reaching home after a journey to foreign lands. Marching to Northampton by a roundabout route did not seem to distress anyone. *"If we are doing nothing else, we're learning geography," said someone.* It was obvious all 115 men remained fit and suntanned by the experience. The 'General' remarked, *"They are as tough and tanned as leather!"* [48]

In fact the road to Chesham was a deliberate diversion from the direct route to Northampton, partly because there was a boot and shoe industry in the country town, and also because several of the men had friends and relatives there. The first stop was at Rickmansworth where bread, cheese and minerals were provided by the Galley army leather contractors. The countryside along the road to Chesham contained attractive scenery but the roads were very dusty. A good shower of rain was needed to make the journey easier, however there were few clouds in the sky. Only one rest was allowed at the Bedford Arms at Chenies (an estate village belonging to the Duke of Bedford). So on to Chesham where the townspeople had been advised by the town crier of the imminent arrival of the Raunds strikers. A good number of adults and children welcomed the little army when they arrived at 6 p.m. The Co-operative Hall was the venue for tea and later, a more substantial meal. For the first time since leaving Raunds there was no evening meeting, instead the Chesham Silver Prize Band volunteered to play in the Market Place while the collectors went about their business. Donations of all sizes had continued to pour in since leaving London. Most of the men decided to visit the local theatre to watch the play entitled "Called Back" which turned out to be a melodrama containing four murders. [49]*Someone joked, "Plenty of work for Morris, our ambulance man."* Which emphasised the fact that very few injuries had occurred needing medical attention, the exception being the bandage for the 'General's ankle.

On the Tuesday night everyone managed as usual to find a bed – some with friends and relatives – as Chesham had some links with Raunds. By 9 a.m. the next morning the march recommenced with Pearson striding out bravely at first. A brake had by now arrived from Raunds which accompanied the men to the end of their march. Although Mr. Gribble's ankle was much better, he rode in the brake for the day and Pearson also had a lift up the hills. The trek through the Chiltern Hills was maintained through the village of Wigginton and Rothchild's Park where the main interest was in seeing deer and kangaroos. The weather became very hot during the morning and everyone was quite exhausted on reaching Tring. Not withstanding their tiredness, after a rest, some washing of socks, and a feed of bread and cheese at the Robin Hood hotel, many felt refreshed enough to visit the local museum. Almost a full complement resumed the long tramp to Leighton Buzzard at 1.45 p.m. although a few men were left behind, still engrossed in the museum, and caught up later.

Only one halt was made during the afternoon and that at Cheddington for a mere fifteen minutes. Despite their best efforts, however, they did not reach journey's end until almost 8 p.m. Very few people turned out to watch the arrival which was just as well, for the marchers had suffered from the hot sun during the afternoon and were somewhat ragged and weary. It was welcome news that the Nonconformist Churches were providing tea in the Temperance Hall, because the intense heat had rendered the day's march the most trying so far experienced. The tiredness of the strikers was compounded by finding more difficulty in obtaining beds than at any place previously. In spite of these problems the usual speeches of welcome, made by four Nonconformist ministers, were received cordially. Mr. Gribble voiced the thanks of the men in his customary manner before the band led the way to a public meeting in the Market-place.

When Thursday morning dawned, it was evident everyone had been provided with bed and board. Following the previous hard day, the projected departure time of 7 a.m. was revised, and at 7.35 a.m. the band struck up and led the little army forward towards Newport Pagnell. The plan was to stop for a meeting at Bletchley Park but, owing to a misunderstanding, this did not materialise. The marchers then continued to Fenny Stratford which they reached at 10.45a.m. Here a splendid meal supplied by Mr P. Mortimer of the Avenue Hotel, Kettering, was taken at 12 noon.

The procession towards Newport was made in fine style keeping up a pace of four miles an hour. It is worth mentioning here, the strong competition among the marchers as to which company strode out the best. Each company took it in turns to lead the way, the members boasting that they had achieved the best style. During the course of the afternoon, a cable was received from Mr. Samuel Taylor, a wellwisher :-

[50]*"Am proud of you and may God bless the men. Say to Gribble he can now write Caesar's Carthage despatch. 'Veni vidi vici'."*[50a]

At Newport the reception was as good as any previously experienced, with a well-known Liberal Mr. A. Bullard kindly providing tea on his lawn at Tichford House. A meeting was held in the evening in order to make the objects of the march known, and to find volunteers who would supply beds. As usual, offers of accommodation were quickly pledged so that no-one had ever needed to sleep in the open since the party left Raunds.

On Friday morning, the penultimate day of the great trek to London town and back, the march did not commence until 10 a.m. as the distance to Northampton was only 14 miles. Prior to departure, it was announced that the arrangements for Saturday would be as follows :- *"Leave Northampton 6 a.m., Wellingborough 11, arrive Rushden 2.30, leave 4.30, arrive Raunds 5.45 p.m."* It was also made known that the total amount collected 'en route' so far, less expenses, was £150. Additional information about the War Office Inquiry was made available to the men and accompanying press representatives, to the effect that

Part 5: THE RETURN TO RAUNDS

it would be conducted by Mr. G.R. Askwith, K.C. He had already met with Mr. W.B. Hornidge, general secretary of the N.U.B.S.O., and arranged to meet Mr. C. Freak the General President, at Leicester to discuss procedure.

[51]*"After being feted and lionised in London, the reception of the Raunds strikers in Northampton must have struck them as decidedly tame - - -. In fact, when, headed by their band and a few of the local trades union officials, they marched up Bridge Street into the Drapery, there was an entire absence of the cheering crowds which in so many places had lined the route."* The reason for the lack of enthusiasm is not easily explained, although it is probable the earlier than expected arrival was a contributory factor. Gribble, when questioned much later, would not agree that the Northampton boot and shoe workers welcomed the Raunds men in a less than wholehearted manner.

The men halted on the Market Square where the 'General' spoke briefly to a crowd of workers who had just finished their week's labour. Luncheon was taken at the Friendly Societies Club after which the men were dismissed for the afternoon which many spent resting, although others went sightseeing or visiting the barbers in preparation for the final trek home. At 8 p.m. the customary evening meeting was held around the fountain in the Market Place. On this occasion there was no band in attendance but a large concourse of people turned up to hear speeches from Councillor Gribble, who had a seat on the borough council and was well known, Councillor Dan. Stanton J.P. and Mr G.E. Robbins who was the president of the Trades Council. The collectors were well patronised to the extent that on reaching Raunds, there was in excess of £200 above expenditure.

The departure from Northampton had been scheduled for 6

a.m. on Saturday, the 20th May, however it was nearly 7 a.m. before they were ready to leave Abington Square. A grey and cheerless morning greeted the marchers as they set off along Wellingborough Road, but a fairly large number of people waved them off, accompanied by Councillor Stanton and Alderman Poulton, representing organised Labour in Northampton. These and other stalwarts led the way to the borough boundary before leaving the little army to continue homeward. On this last stage of their adventure, because the weather was not so warm, the men marched briskly along looking dusty but happy to be nearing journey's end, and setting a brisker pace than hitherto.

A first stop was made at the curiously named inn, the World's End, at Ecton. Soon they were off again heading for Wilby, whistling and singing well known songs to the accompaniment of a mouth organ played by one of the band. A favourite air seemed to be, 'The Red Flag'. While in Northampton one of those who had decided to get his hair cut and have a shave was scandalised having been charged ninepence. Another misfortune occurred at Newport Pagnell when a marcher from Ringstead slipped from a curbstone and injured his ankle. For most of the twenty miles home the wagonette had perforce to carry one more passenger.

As they entered the village of Wilby, the order was given to form fours and the stopping place at The George was reached in fine style. Here many locals were waiting intent on asking the strikers how they felt after their long hike. To these queries the men usually replied, *"As fit as anything"*, and *"Beautiful"*. One of the intrepid footsloggers held up his handsewn army boots for inspection by the crowd – the kind of footwear which was the subject of the dispute. Despite walking to London and back, they were only worn at the tip and looked fit to be worn for several more marches.

Wellingborough was reached at 11 a.m., surrounded by several hundreds of shoehands who had met the little army at Wilby. The band played a march entitled 'Never behind', all the way until a halt was called at the Victoria Inn. A crowd of a thousand or more gathered at the Liberal Club where the marchers had a wash before enjoying a lunch of bread, cheese and pickles provided by the local branch of the N.U.B.S.O. Some familiar faces to the men were mingled in the cheering throng, since several wives and sweethearts had journeyed to Wellingborough to meet their spouses and follow them home.

The few miles to Rushden via Little Irchester were soon traversed and, shortly after 2 p.m., they marched into the town with a splendid swing. Reaching the Oakley Arms, they turned left down Washbrook Road to be met by the Rushden Volunteer and the Higham Ferrers Silver Bands. After a wash at the Trades Union Club, a crowd of between 2,000 and 3,000 people heard speeches of welcome from Mr C. Bates and Comrade Rose Jarvis of Northampton. The latter was an impassioned address, declaring that Comrade Gribble, in his protest at the House of Commons, had greatly advanced the principles of Socialism and Labour.

[52]'The Red Flag' was sung by Comrade Frank Clark. There followed a sumptuous tea in the club after which 'General' Gribble took the opportunity to thank the people of Rushden and Higham for a splendid welcome back. [53]*"We have become accustomed to hearty receptions but you have given us the heartiest of all,"* he exclaimed.

Before leaving Rushden the marchers paraded the town and left for Raunds, and home, just before 5 p.m. headed by the two bands. A halt was called at Higham Ferrers Square where another large crowd was waiting. Speaking from the Market Cross Mr. Bazeley and Councillor Gribble thanked the inhabitants of the ancient borough for their support and sympathy. Then, with the Higham band again accompanying the strikers on their homeward journey, at least as far as the borough boundary, the march became more of a procession. From Rushden onwards the men were joined by friends and relatives travelling on foot, or on cycles, together with several heavily laden brakes bringing up the rear.

It seemed that, as the day for the return of the heroes drew near, the announcement of the final arrangements was eagerly awaited, and when it was found the chief demonstration on the last day would take place at Rushden (the headquarters of the local branch of the Union), large numbers decided to join in the welcome there. Accordingly, very soon after midday on Saturday, a stream of traffic set out with the object of meeting up with the heroes in the larger town. There were brakes and wagonettes conveying the female relatives of the strikers, and other vehicles of various descriptions, besides a constant succession of cyclists, not only from Raunds, but from many parts of the district. As the afternoon wore on it became generally known that the men would not reach Raunds until after 6 o'clock, but long before that hour the town was all astir. Parties who had been to Rushden were returning in advance of the main body, whilst others were on their way to meet them. [54]Indeed, it seemed as if the whole population turned out to witness the arrival. In the current division of feeling in Raunds a united welcome was of course out of the question, but everyone appeared to be interested in the main event of the day. Many of the houses at the entrance to the town, and also others leading to the Woodbine Club, had small flags hung out; and one of these, near the Hall, had 'WELCOME' inscribed on it –

probably none the less genuine for being unpretentious.

The men, having left Northampton at 7 a.m. on their last day's tramp – a distance of 22 miles – did the final stage from Higham without a pause; and at a good swinging pace, preceded and followed by vehicles, and accompanied by hundreds of people. They looked bronzed and hardened, and strengthened by their march. On nearing Stanwick, Pearson the cripple who had been riding, resumed his position at the head of the column. His fame had gone before him, and as he stumped pluckily along on his new crutches he came in for a large share of attention. Mr Gribble still limping from his recent sprain, and using a stick, walked alongside the men. After so many speeches and following a bad cold he had very little voice left, but maintained he was in capital health.

[55]On the way to Stanwick, Mr Gribble spoke to newspaper reporters and answered their questions :-

"The behaviour of the men had been excellent and there had been no cause of complaint. He did not understand what he had seen in the newspapers about the proposed settlement. He wanted to see something official before he was prepared to discuss it. Alluding to the march itself, he said the men had done about 160 miles, and not one had fallen out until that morning when one man rode a little way from Northampton owing to an injury sustained at Newport Pagnell. The men said they were getting used to marching, and that the second day was the worst. They mentioned that the only rain to fall was on Trafalgar Square, and there had often been a longing for a shower to lay the dust."

Before Stanwick, the strikers began singing the 'Red Flag' again, and on entering the village the band played 'Never behind'. People called out, *"There's Gribble"*, and *"Good old Gribble"*, while a child called out, *"Dad"*, and received a smile in return.

Part 5: THE RETURN TO RAUNDS

With half a mile to go to the Red Lion crossroads the band struck up another march, 'Black Brunswicker', as along the route from the public house and down Wellington Hill groups of people cheered the returning heroes. Straight on they marched, the men singing again with the chief sentiment, 'Dear old Raunds' (though to what tune is not recorded). One of the loudest cheers came from a crowd gathered outside the Coffee Tavern and Liberal Institute in Brook Street as the little army, with heads held high, passed the post office clock registering 6.24 p.m. and approached the Square to the sound of the band playing an appropriate finale, 'Never behind'.

A huge concourse was gathering at the Square to honour the return, estimated by many at five thousand, which would have been more than the total population. 'General' Gribble could not but pronounce a final speech ignoring the hoarseness of his voice; he addressed the men as "Comrades" and gave a summary of the previous two weeks' events :-

[56] *"He said that although Mr Arnold Forster refused to meet them, they had brought the attention of the country – (Hear, hear) – to the anomalies under the fair wages clause, and he felt confident that as a result of their march the current rate of wage would be replaced by the trade union rate (Hear, hear and applause). They won their first victory when they got the inquiry —— and their demonstration had forced the hands of the government to grant the review.*

The men who went to London with him had been good, staunch, sober, honest, industrious workmen (Loud applause). They had won golden opinions everywhere they went. He had no complaints in the least of any insobriety on the part of any one man

Returning home on 20th May 1905. The square at Raunds was crowded with people to greet the marchers. A short meeting was held and then "General" Gribble was carried shoulder-high to the Woodbine Club.

– (Hear, hear) – nor of the want of discipline in any one man.

He said they had done gloriously in London – (So you have). They had shown the people of England that right in the heart of Northamptonshire there were little places called Raunds and Ringstead – (Hear, hear) – which could show the world when necessary, they knew how to organise and how to demonstrate - -

Part 5: THE RETURN TO RAUNDS

that when they had wrongs they would show the people how to right them.

He said the march had been as good as a holiday – and had done them all more good than a month at the seaside (Laughter and applause).

He noticed in the Press that there was some talk of 2s.5d. being recognised as the current rate for making a pair of boots (Cries of 'Shame' and 'Never, won't have it'). He was certainly not prepared to believe the officials of the union would be so silly as to accept that. They'd had a good fight so far, they had fought it well, and they were going to fight it to the finish (Applause).

He wanted to thank the Press and the police for the splendid way in which they had helped them both upward to town and homeward. He picked out the 'Daily News' for special mention for their good reports and also for the donation of a cheque for £50.

He would publish accounts of money received and paid out at a meeting in the Club at 11 a.m. on Monday next."

With that the speech concluded and Mr. Gribble was carried shoulder high to the Woodbine Club, although a number of supporters on the Square continued to debate the events of the previous fortnight for many more hours.

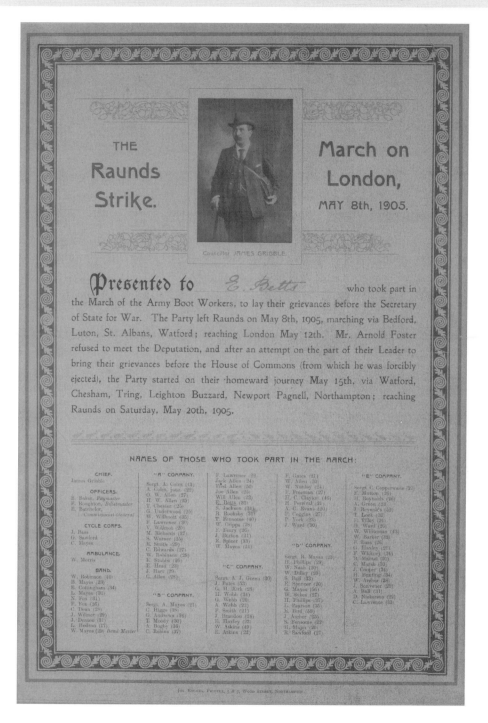

Part 5: THE RETURN TO RAUNDS

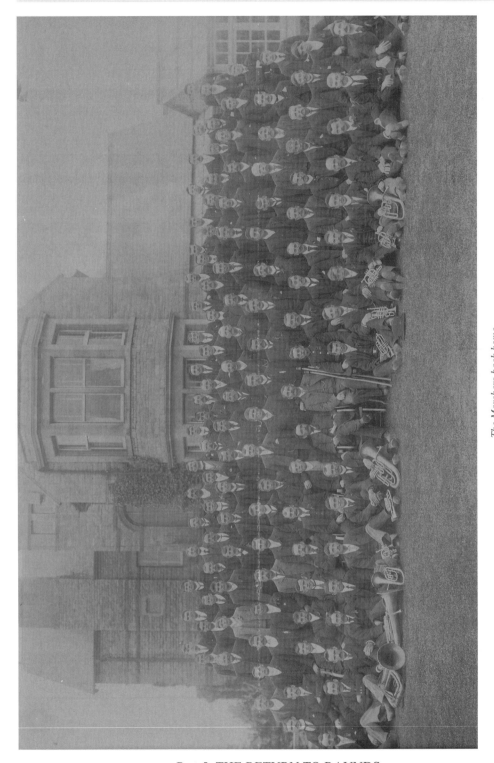

The Marchers back home.

Monies collected 'en route' enabled every marcher to be presented with a large copy of this photograph.

Part 5: THE RETURN TO RAUNDS

THE INQUIRY AND OTHER RESULTS

On Monday May 22nd, the strike continuing, most of the marchers went back to picket duty, although after an eleven week struggle the dispute in the army boot trade in Raunds and district appeared to be within sight of a satisfactory settlement. Mr. G.R. Askwith, K.C. appointed by the Army Council to conduct an inquiry, wasted no time on the matter. Already, on Friday May 19th a meeting had been held at Leicester between both sides of the industry; Mr. John T. Hawthorne of Finedon and Mr. Harry Nichols of Kettering represented the manufacturers, and Mr. Chas. Freak and Mr. W.B. Hornidge, the general president and general secretary of the Shoe Operatives' Union, were the men's representatives. This was the beginning of some long and protracted negotiations which continued at the Queen Victoria Hotel, Rushden, on Tuesday May 23rd.

After long deliberations the conference submitted two statements of prices, one to apply for the remainder of current contracts and the other for contracts in 1906. Both these statements were placed before separate meetings of manufacturers and strikers to try to obtain approval. It quickly became clear to the employees that if they returned to work accepting these conditions, they would immediately be in a worse situation, although in the following year a statement of 2s 11d. per pair for boots made should apply. Despite the General President of the Union arguing they had secured a victory in principle, since a proper statement of prices was secured, the Union officials were instructed to press for the full 1906 statement to be paid at once.

A new proposal from the manufacturers offering an increase of a penny a pair from 1905, was rejected by a meeting of strikers voting overwhelmingly by ballot 304 votes to 31. Further concessions were made by both sides, with an Arbitrator being influential in bringing about a final settlement which allowed the men to resume work after a thirteen week stoppage. [57]An important development was the setting up of a Board of Conciliation and Arbitration to resolve future difficulties in the district. Additionally, it was agreed that no victimisation of strikers should take place.

The dispute cost the Union well over £2,000, but it was agreed the expenditure had been worth while, particularly as the Army boot work was now to be organised on a fair and equitable basis. As Mr. F.A. Channing M.P. wrote in a letter to the Secretary of State for War; [58] *"The decision to send Mr. Askwith down – has led to the happiest results - , and has thus, I trust, laid the firm foundation of permanent peace and efficient working of the contract system."*

At the end of the dispute each of the marchers received a handsome framed certificate in commemoration of the great event. Surmounted by a photograph of Mr. Gribble the inscription outlines the story of the march and also contains a full list of names of those who took part. A large framed photograph of the men who took part, and including Pearson the cripple, was also presented, together with a framed paper memorial of the rally in Trafalgar Square.

In spite of the march to London not being in the minute records of the Rushden branch of N.U.B.S.O.,[59] the September report states that Councillor J. Gribble was presented with a marble clock, value £6-6s, subscribed by 300 Army workers, for his valuable services as dispute manager during the late strike. Gribble undoubtedly made history in the way he assembled his 'troops' and stimulated national interest and sympathy for the cause. The Raunds March was not the first or the last of its kind – but it was one of the first to reach its objectives as an organised body. Most notably the strike and the march won the principle which had been sought – a standard rate of pay accepted and enforced by the War Office.[60]

It might be well to let the 'Northampton Mercury' have the last word, especially since their reporter had not been fully convinced of the efficacy of the project when, on May 8th, the marchers set out for London town. Here is the gist of the paper's report as published on Friday, May 19th :-

[61] *"It is long since a Northamptonshire demonstration has occupied so large an amount of public attention as the march of the Raunds strikers to London and back. There has been something so vivid and picturesque about the demonstration that the public eye has been captivated from start to finish. The bold sturdiness, which was willing to tramp in mass for ninety miles to lay grievances before the governing authorities of the Empire, has especially appealed to people all over the country. It required no small measure of Northamptonshire 'grit' to face the difficulties of a march to London – and – the event has been the topic of sympathetic comment in nearly every home and in almost every newspaper in the country. The continental papers have given long accounts, for the whole thing is so insular that it strikes the European mind as expressly noteworthy. The leading facts have been cabled to every important newspaper in all quarters of the globe, and to some of the Atlantic liners a thousand miles at sea,*

the Marconigram[62] carried the news."

As a postscript, it is worth recalling that although Raunds was known as 'Red Raunds', throughout the county and beyond for several years after the happenings recorded here, the boot and shoe trade prospered in the town for many more decades. The setting up of an arbitration board, mentioned previously, meant there were very few disputes between manufacturers and employees, any that did occur were settled quickly. Therefore it is unfortunate the bright optimism of the men who returned from London in 1905 could not be carried into the twenty first century, since the last boot and shoe factory closed in 1999. Nevertheless, the spirit of 1905 still permeates the inhabitants of today, and it is fitting that past endeavours should be charted and commemorated in the year 2005.

Notes

Details of printed material given here in abbreviated form will be found in the list of Reference Books and Local Sources.

Title page : The name Raunds is given as Randes and Raundes in medieval documents – locally pronounced 'Rance', or even 'Rarnce', until very recent times.

1   Ireson, Northamptonshire, p.188

2   Hatley, Shoemakers in Northamptonshire (1762-1911), p.17

3   The London Gazette, Sept.15, 1829, p.1718

4   P. Roberts, private research

5   The name 'Nichols' also given as 'Nicholls'

6   Letter in 'The Co-operator', 1st June 1867

7   Hall, Harding & Putt, Raunds Picturing the Past, p.157

8   Ibid

9   Fox, History of N.U.B.S.O., 1958

10 Ibid, p.202

11 Quoted from Raunds Parish Church Magazine, 1904

12 Allen and Bartley, An Epic of Trade Unionism, p.36

13 Ibid

14 Ibid, p.38

15 N.P.P. 1981-82, Brooker, James Gribble & Raunds Strike, Quotes Manchester Guardian, March 23

16 Wellingborough News, Frid. March 10, 1905.

17 Allen & Bartley, p.38

17a Allen & Bartley, p.38

18 N.R.O., Northampton Mercury, March 24, 1905.

19 Wellingborough News, March 17, 1905.

20 Ibid.

21 Northampton Mercury, April 21 (See Appendices)

22 Allen and Bartley, p.40 and Wellingborough News, May 5.

23 Allen and Bartley, p.41

24 N.R.O., N'pton Mercury, May 12

25 Wellingborough News, May12 (from Kettering Evening Telegraph)

26 N.P.P., Brooker, Quote from N'pton Daily Chronicle.

27 Bedfordshire Times, May 12 and Bedford Record, May 9

28 Wellingborough News, May12.

29 Ibid.

30 Ibid

31 N.P.P., Brooker, p.282.

32 Wellingborough News, May 12

33 Watford Observer, May 13

33a Ibid also Allen and Bartley, Epic, p.43

34 Wellingborough News, May 19

35 Allen & Bartley

36 Wellingborough News, May 19

37 D.N.B. gives more details of career as Trade Union activist

38 Daily News, May 13, Quote in N.P.P., Brooker, also Wellingborough News, May 19etc.

39 The Times, May 9, Quote in N.P.P.,Brooker.

40 Ibid, May 11

41 Thrapston, Raunds and Oundle Journal, May 28,1937, Quote in Fox, History of N.U.B.S.O., p.288

42 N.P.P.,Brooker, p.284
43 Report in most national and local press. Speech by Keir Hardie father of the Labour Party.
44 In the 1906 General Election the Conservative government gave way to a Liberal administration. 50 Labour M.P.s were elected which was the largest number up to that time.
45 Wellingborough News, May 19
46 N.P.P., Brooker, Quote from N'pton Daily Reporter, May 15
47 Wellingborough News, May 19
48 Ibid
49 Ibid
50 Ibid
50a Veni, vidi, vici (Latin) = I came, I saw, I conquered – usually ascribed to Julius Caesar but the derivation is of doubtful authenticity.
51 Report from Wellingborough News, May 26 (taken from Kettering Evening Telegraph and other newspapers May 19, May 20)
52 Allen and Bartley,Epic, p.44
53 Wellingborough News, March 26
54 Ibid
55 Ibid. as reported in the local evening and weekly press.
56 Ibid. extracts from newspaper reporters' accounts
57 N.P.P., Brooker, p.285
58 Allen and Bartley, Epic, p.46
59 50th Anniversary booklet, 1955, p.11
60 Fox, History of N.U.B.S.O., p.289
61 Northampton Mercury, May 19
62 Marconigram = wireless telegraph only recently invented.

NOTES

Reference Books and Local Sources

Allen A.C. and Bartley C.J., An Epic of Trade Unionism, 1934

50th Anniversary Programme, April 30th 1955, N.U.B.S.O.

Betts J.R., The Raunds Strike and March to London 1905, Raunds and District History Society, 1989 and 1991

Brooker K., James Gribble and the Raunds Strike of 1905, Northamptonshire Past and Present, Northamptonshire Record Society, 1981/82

Dictionary of National Biography (Concise), Oxford University Press, 1994

Fox A., A History of the National Union of Boot and Shoe Operatives 1874 - 1957, Blackwell, Oxford, 1958

Hall D., Harding R. and Putt C., Raunds Picturing the Past, March and Buscott, 1988

Hatley V.A., Shoemakers in Northamptonshire 1762 - 1911, A Statistical Survey, Northampton Historical Series, 1971

Ireson T., Northamptonshire, County Series, Hale, 1954

Roberts P., Unpublished research from London Gazette

The Co-operator, Journal of the Co-operative Movement, 1867

Various monthly reports, N.U.B.S.O., Rushden Branch

Newspapers and periodicals in order of first reference
(1905 unless stated)

London Gazette, 1829, Sept. 15

Rance Re-viewed, Winter 2003, Letter from Isaac Burton - first published in
The Co-operator June 1, 1867

Raunds Parish Church Magazine, January 1904

Manchester Guardian, March 23

Wellingborough News, March 10, March 17, May 5, May 12, May 19, May 26

Northampton Mercury, March 24, April 21, May 12, May 19

Northampton Daily Chronicle

Bedfordshire Times, May 12

Bedford Record, May 9

West Herts and Watford Observer, May 13

Daily News, May 13

The Times, May 9, May I I

Thrapston, Raunds and Oundle Journal, 1937, May 28

Northampton Daily Reporter, May 15

Kettering Evening Telegraph, May 19, May 20

Other Newspapers consulted or mentioned

Rushden Echo

Rushden Argos

Reynolds News

Morning Post

Bedfordshire Mercury

Luton News

Herts and St. Albans Advertiser

Watford Daily Circular

Luton Reporter

Northampton Daily Echo

Watford Critic

Kettering Leader

Daily Mirror

The Sphere

APPENDIX A

The names and ages of the marchers.

James Gribble
R. Baker, Paymaster
F. Boughton, Billetmaster
E. Batchelor, Commissariat-General
J. Bass, Cycle Corps
G. Sawford, Cycle Corps
C. Mayes, Cycle Corps
W. Morris, Ambulance Sergt.
Sergt. A. Coles (43)
A. Coles, jun. (22)
O. W. Allen (27)
H. W. Allen (25)
T. Chester (25)
G. Underwood (25)
W. Willmot (36)
F. Lawrence (30)
V. Willmott (20)
M. Richards (27)
S. Warmer (26)
R. Smith (29)
C. Edwards (27)
W. Robinson (29)
E. Stubbs (26)
E. Head (23)
J. Heart (29)
C. Allen (28)
Sergt. A. Mayes (21)
C. Higgs (38)
G. Andrews (24)
T. Moody
A. Bugby (36)
C. Robins (37)
F. Lawrence (22)
Jack Allen (24)
Fred Allen (50)
Joe Allen (25)
Will Allen (22)
E. Betts (38)
S. Jackson (34)
R. Rooksby (31)

T. Fensome (40)
W. Cripps (28) Bythorne
F. Tear (26)
J. Burton (21)
E. Spicer (33)
W. Mayers (24)
Sergt. A. J. Green (30)
J. Bates (53)
G. K. Kirk (28)
H. Webb (24)
W. Webb (20)
A. Webb (22)
F. Smith (21)
J. Brandon (24)
E. Haxley (23)
W. Atkins (49)
G. Atkins (22)
F. Gates (22)
W. Allen (20)
W. Nunley (24)
F. Freeman (24)
H. C. Clayton (46)
H. Percival (21)
A. C. Evans (20)
F. Coggins (27)
D. York (23)
J. Ward (30)
Sergt. R. Mayes (23) Ringstead
H. Philips (29) Ringstead
W. Nash (20)
W. Dilley (23)
S. Ball (33) Ringstead
E. Spencer (22) Ringstead
G. Mayes (56) Ringstead
W. Sykes (27) Ringstead
W. Morris (47) Ringstead
H. Phillips (27) Ringstead
L. Pearson (35) Ringstead
E. Bird (59) Ringstead

J. Archer (25) Ringstead
S. Fensome (22) Ringstead
H. Major (20) Ringstead
R. Sawford (27) Ringstead
Sergt. C. Copperwaite (32)
F. Mutton (26)
H. Reynolds (26)
A. Green (23)
J. Reynolds (52)
T. Lock (32)
F. Tilley (31)
H. Ward (26)
W. Whiteman (43)
W. Barker (32)
F. Bass (26)
G. Haxley (21)
F. Whitney (24)
B. Mantell (20)
C. Marsh (30)
J. Cooper (34)
H. Bunting (34)
W. Archer (36)
J. Scrivener (27)
A. Ball (31)
D. Nickerson (22)
C. Lawrence (33)
W. Robinson (40) Ringstead ⎤
B. Mayes (23) Ringstead
E. Collingham (34) Ringstead
L. Mayes (31) Ringstead
N. Fox (31) Ringstead
F. Fox (26) Ringstead
C. Dean (28)
J. Wilmer (29)
J. Denton (31)
L. Hodson (22)
W. Mayes (29) Band Master ⎦

Band

APPENDIX B
Extract from 'The Watford Critic' June, 1905
"LEST WE FORGET"
"The Bootmakers' March"

The men of Raunds they " waxed " wroth,
And thought upon their " feat ",
For though, said they, we're cobblers all,
We can't make both " ends " meet.

We pull and stitch and stitch and pull,
And army " Hoofs we pads ";
But bosses think because we sew
We find no use for " brads ".

For fifteen bob's our weekly wage,
And here we all do swear.
To never more make army boots
At two and six the pair.

And so--our grievances to " heal "
And get our righteous doles-
We'll march away to London town;
We will-upon our " souls ".

Now comrade Gribble he shall be
The leader of our band,
A Blucher or a Wellington
To press our just demand.

They marched-and villages and towns
Received them all " en fete "
And cheered the men who would not stick
To army contract rate.

"LEST WE FORGET" - CONTINUED

They walked along with cheery song,
And never a sigh forlorn,
They never once were needing bread,
They'd often too much " corn ".

Also-although their boots began
To wear-as on they paced.
Yet boots were really thought of last
Although-not always " laced ".

And when great London town they reached,
Although they soon found "bobs"
They found also the War Office
Like Raunds had got its "snobs"

For Ministers, whose duty was
The grievance sore to book.
Thought, on the " whole ", 'twas better for
To take their "button hook"

But yet they did not march in vain,
For Labour's heard the call, And it "
boots " well when Labour is
Prepared to stand by " all ".

And when in future we shall tell
Of the great march that's past.
Let's give the men of Raunds the praise
For sticking to the "last"

APPENDIX B

APPENDIX C

The following was published in the "Rushden Echo"
as the "March of the Strike Brigade"

Forward, Strike Brigade!
Forward through sun and shade
Forward - to London
On through dust and wind they came
Comrades with a single aim
Step by step to world-wide fame,
The fifteen and hundred.
Theirs not to idly sigh,
"We are helpless- hear our cry!"
At Westminster they would try,
Justice to win.
Friends to the right of them,
Friends to the left of them,
Friends all around them,
Helped, cheered and wondered.
How well they stood the test,
Undeterred by capric's jest,
Reached the goal in labour's quest
The fifteen and hundred.
When will the story fade,
Of the splendid march they made?
The march of the Strike Brigade;
The march to London!
Raunds men will long be known,
As Labour heroes, who have shown
That toilers mean, where they have sown,
To claim fair pay-at least their own;
The fifteen and hundred.

APPENDIX D

Extracts from the Northampton Mercury'
and the 'Kettering Leader' of 1905.

N.M. April 7. On April 4 at Thrapston Magistrate Court:

Edward Nunley and Hewitt Bates, two youths aged 14 and 16, summoned for besetting house of Eliza Richardson with a view to compel her to abstain from working as a hand stabber at Messrs. Lawrence and Co. on March 21.

John Askham. Frederick Freeman, William Francis Harvey, Albert Mayes, William Whiteman, Charles Higgs and Hairy Sanders shoe operatives charged with persistently following George Henry Roberts [1] (of Ringstead with a view to compel him to abstain from working as a shoemaker for Messrs. Lawrence and Co. on March 29. (A police sergeant and ten constables had had to escort Roberts home accompanied by 200 men, women and children).

K.L. April 7. Raunds Strike. Thrapston Police Court Proceedings.

First Case: Fred Phillips of Ringstead summoned for intimidating George Henry Roberts, shoemaker, Ringstead with a view to compel him to abstain from working as a shoemaker for Messrs. Lawrence and Co. at Raunds on March 17. Complainant was NOT a member of the Union.

Complainant said he met Phillips - a picket - near the factory. The latter said. 'You won't bring any work out today George.'

Witness made no reply. He went into the factory, got his work Out, and put it in a sack on his back. Defendant called him a 'scabby b -------' and said, 'You had better look out, you will meet someone.

Defendant said that his words were misquoted he actually said, 'Well George, are you going to bring any work out today?' He did not say, 'You won't bring any work out'.
He had been friends with Roberts and was now. When Roberts came out of the factory he said, 'Well George, I'm surprised at you bringing work out. I should have thought you would be the last man to do so'. He did not use any threats at all

1. Roberts was a relative of Margaret Thatcher's father, Alfred.

APPENDIX D Continued

Next Case: Joseph Archer, Ralph Mayes. Henry Major, Harry Wood, Fred Fox, Hermin Baker and John Gray, shoehands of Ringstead were summoned for besetting the house of George Henry Roberts, shoemaker, Ringstead, with a view to compel him to abstain from working as a shoemaker for Messrs. Lawrence and Co. of Raunds at Ringstead on March 17. All pleaded not guilty.

Offence occurred (according to Mr. Simpsom prosecuting) at about 6.45 a crowd of about 200 assembled in front of the house, shouting and beating tin cans. The constable in charge (P.C.Sullivan) had to telegraph for assistance and stated crowd were rattling and beating cans, hooting, booing, shouting and appeared in an excited state. P.C. Parrish came to his assistance but disturbance continued about three hours. Inspector Butlin and other officers also arrived.

William Jackson (aged 13) said at five o'clock on the day in question he was in a football field on the Denford Road. He saw Ralph Mayes, who said 'get the tins ready; Roberts has taken work out'.

Mary Elizabeth Roberts, wife of the complainant, said she was a hand stabber at Ringstead. She was at home on the day in question, and just as she had lit the lamp she heard the 'tin kettle band' coming.

Defendant Baker said he went to see the tin-kettling. 'He did not believe in people working when others were on strike. He would swear he had never hooted that evening'. Phillips, Archer and others gave similar evidence. Defendant Fox said he heard the tin-kettling, so went to see what was going on. Roberts' own children had got tin kettles. P.C. Sullivan shook a child and the crowd hooted.

William Roberts, complainant's own brother, said he had a conversation with Gray, who did not make any disturbance at all. Cyril Peacock said he saw no disturbance - Harry Sibley gave similar evidence.

Bench fined Phillips £ 1 with 6s costs. Others fined 2s-6d. each.

APPENDIX D Continued

N.M. April 21

William Wileman was charged that on March 29 he intimidated Walter Knighton on the way home from Adams' factory with a crowd of 130.
Defendant said 'How do you like being taken home by a policeman?
If I had a gun I would shoot you'. Knighton was not a member of the Union.

On being found guilty the defendant was fined ten shillings or in default fourteen days hard labour. Wileman elected to go to prison.

APPENDIX E

LIST OF SURVIVORS OF THE HISTORIC MARCH

April 30th, 1955

J. Archer, High Street, Ringstead.

J. Allen, 12 Dillington, Great Staughton, Kimbolton.

O. W. Allen, 187 London Road, Bedford.

H. W. Allen, 4 Wellington Road, Raunds.

J. Bass, 2 Edgar Road, Kettering.

A. C. Evans, 108 Greasboro' Road, Rotherham, Yorks.

S. Fensome, High Street, Ringstead.

E. Haxley, 5 Gladstone Street, Raunds.

G. Haxley, 38 Wimbledon Street, Northampton.

L. Hodson, Highlands, Finham, Coventry.

C. Lawrence, 14 Marshalls Road, Raunds.

B. Mantle, 15 Midland Road, Thrapston.

A. Mayes, 60 Marshalls Road, Raunds.

B. Mayes, 13 Primrose Hill, Raunds.

W. Mayes, 3 Spresser Street, North Ipswich, Queensland, Australia.

W. Nash, High Street, Ringstead.

W. Nunley, 43 Thorpe Street, Raunds.

H. Percival, 139 Eastern Avenue North, Northampton.

E. Phillips, Ashfields Cottage, Brook Street, Raunds.

H. Phillips, 3 Wentworth Road, Rushden.

F. Roughton, 37 Thorpe Street, Raunds.

M. Richards, 44 High Street, Raunds.

J. Scrivener, 28 Brook Street, Raunds.

W. Sykes, 38 Halford Road, Thrapston.

G. Underwood, Northampton.

A. Webb, 23 Red Row, Raunds.

V. Wilmott, 38 Marshalls Road, Raunds.

P. York, 13 Park Avenue, Raunds.